Co.... Yourself In

Let's Eat!

Lesley Ann Taylor Ph.D

Dedicated to my parents, Eryl and Pamela Jenkins

For my father,
my inspiration, my friend and my benefactor.
I miss you.

For my mother,
who in cooking and in life always told me I could.

Having something to share around

Once upon a time

I overheard a mother explaining to her child

– mine means I have something to share –

simple yet profound

the more goodies you create
the more goodies you have to share around

Thanks to:
Dave, my husband, soulmate and fellow traveller with whom I share so many public and private adventures (most of which we'll keep to ourselves). Thank you for being a winner for me. I love you.

Our kids, Joel, Jemma, Martha, Leah, Samuel, Tobias and Keziah. Next to your Dad you have been life's biggest gift to me. Thank you for individually and collectively and consistently pointing me in the way of caring. I love you all.

Our daughter-in-law Kady, who sparkles so gently in our midst. Thank you for giving me space to grow into the mother-in-law I want to be. I love you too.

Stanislas, Elise, Audrey, Andrea, Marie and Tom, Louis, Jean and Marie, Martina, Cyrielle and Emma, who each came into our family to be loved (you are), to call us Mum and Dad and to learn our language. Thanks for stretching me to be worthy of you and shaping my language to be clear and simple. And Stanislas, remember the day, when after some new mischief of yours, I said - whatever you do Stan - I'll still say you are my son. I learnt something about depths of love that day - I hope you did too.

My energy to write has come out of my remarkable relationships with all of you. Thank you.

"I came that **you** might have life,
and might have it abundantly."[1]

Jesus Christ

---

[1] Paraphrased from John 10:10, the Bible.

Count Yourself In - Let's Eat

The remarkable cooking coach
that enables you
to seize the choice that is yours
to use what you've got
to get what you want

This Choice is Yours!

Contents

Sweet Yummies 81

This Choice is Yours! 106

Count Yourself In

Part I - PURPOSE

This book is about creating remarkable results from ordinary things

The adventure begins in a cookbook and moves out into life

Count Yourself In

Setting you free

This is a cookbook about choice. There are no recipes to follow with exact quantities and mixes. Instead, Cooking Catalysts offer you cooking adventures that keep creating space for you to choose.

A catalyst is something that precipitates a change. The Cooking Catalysts are here to precipitate changes in your thinking, cooking, and living.

The word catalyst derives from the Greek 'kataluein' meaning 'to loosen' or, as I like to think of it, 'to set free'.

Out of the ordinary

You can create remarkable eats
from whatever your starting point
as an ordinary person, in an ordinary place,
with ordinary foodstuff

Along the way as you think and play
you'll catch glimpses of something bigger;
the adventure of creating a remarkable life
from whatever your starting point
as an ordinary person, in an ordinary place,
with ordinary stuff

Playing into more choice

Playing into more choice in cooking involves working with an assortment of Cooking Catalysts that give you just enough information to get going. What fascinates you may not be the thing that fascinates someone else and so the book remains free from lots of interesting details about food and cooking that you can find elsewhere.

Instead you learn, for example, that bread making involves flour, liquid, and something to make it rise. Then you play around with some flour, water, and yeast, with a little sugar, salt, and oil and have a go. After that you learn how Cinnamon Rolls and Iced Buns can be derived from the bread dough, with just a little extra sugar and some eggs and milk to soften the texture. Your attention is drawn to what's the same, to what has changed, and to what is different in the result. Then with those ideas in mind, you play around and design your own buns and your own bread. Pizza also comes out of bread dough. Just add tomato and cheese to the bread base and you can put anything else, or everything else, or nothing else at all, on top!

The Cooking Catalysts take what might be complex and make it something simple so you can create your own simple and different eats, or create more complex combinations!

You'll find a Cooking Catalyst for simple soup made with water and vegetables (any vegetables you want). And if you want to create a more complex soup you'll find the way. You are set free to use your ideas to create your own eats.

Near the back you'll find the Sweet Yummies. Check out the Chocolate Brownies (of course, if you are out of chocolate you can make vanilla ones, or orange ones, or whatever you choose -- just call them Blondies). In just over half an hour you can have enough Brownies or Blondies for you and your friends!

In short, this book focuses on simple principles around putting food together. Cooking Catalysts set you free for adventures with ordinary things that lead you to simply make something remarkable and say with a certain boldness...

Let's Eat!

Count Yourself In - Let's Eat
More than a way of cooking, it's a way of life

So, the purpose of this book is to help you begin to make more choices. It's about,

You taking **Your** food in **Your** kitchen to create something **You** want to eat!

As you think into these choices you can release yourself even further into a confident freedom to keep choosing for yourself, to keep moving forward into more, and to keep changing ordinary things into the remarkable.   And when it keeps happening in your kitchen you'll find it begins to happen in other areas of your life too until Count Yourself In becomes your lifestyle choice with remarkable results.

Count Yourself In - Let's Eat
It's a great way to begin to learn about creating a remarkable life

Part II - PARADIGM for a Feast of Choice

Here is the big picture of the game

Count Yourself In is a way of thinking
into choice and participation
to increase your remarkable results from wherever
you begin

You learn to give yourself
permission to write your own recipes-
-And maybe Count Yourself In is your training for
understanding how you can give yourself
permission to write your own life

Best of all...

You step in and make remarkable feasts from
ordinary things-
-And maybe Count Yourself In is your training for
making for yourself, from any ordinary beginning,
a remarkable life

This Choice Is Yours!

Count Yourself In

As you move into this Feast of Choice paradigm
you may find yourself thinking differently
into choice
into cooking
and into life

And you take the following steps...

First, you choose to be the one to choose
Second, you choose what you want
Third, you choose to make your choice happen

Stepping up to choose to choose

Your power **to choose to choose** is affected by the thoughts you think, the words you chatter to yourself, and the habits that are part of what you do every day.

Counting Yourself In: Choosing thinking that works

Your thinking affects your attitudes, and your attitudes affect your success, so how you think matters. Take for example your thinking around something that didn't work out as planned. Your thinking in response to that disappointment will shape how you feel about the rest of your day and, having shaped your feelings, will then shape your actions. Imagine you add too much water to a curry and it has become thin soup. An unhelpful thinking-start is:

"The food is a failure... I am a failure."

"I'll never be able to cook... I'll stop trying."

Now you are stopped!

Instead, choose more useful **thinking-starts**:

There is no failure only feedback

With this thinking-start you can ask --

"How can I use this feedback to take me closer to a way that works?"

You are now going forwards!

It is better to increase your number of choices
With this thinking-start you can ask --
"How can I increase the number of choices I have around overcoming the challenge I face?"
You are now going forwards!

You already have all the resources you need
With this thinking-start you can ask --
"How will I use the resources available to me for success?"
You are now going forwards!

Help your thinking to help you move forwards!

Make a move - in large letters write out these thinking-starts and post them on your wall

---

Counting Yourself In: Choosing chatter that works

Your chatter to yourself speaks to your subconscious and what you do subconsciously affects your success. Take for example something you do every day, like getting dressed. It works a bit like this. You decide to get dressed and then without much conscious thought about how to put your legs into your trousers or skirt, and your arms into your shirt, you find you have done it. It happens because your subconscious mind is able to do certain things while freeing you up to focus on doing some other things at the same time. That's how people who drive cars can control the car (brake, change gear, steer) while talking. That's how you make a coffee, butter the bread, or do whatever it is you do easily and often without much conscious thought.

However, when you hear, 'Don't think about a purple pig', then you probably do exactly the opposite and a purple pig arrives at the centre of your thinking. Your subconscious mind has only registered 'think about a purple pig'. If you want your subconscious mind to work with you then it is useful to understand that your subconscious mind ignores negatives.

So, when commanding your subconscious mind to work with you, it is more effective to chatter to yourself, 'remember the salt', than to chatter to yourself, 'don't forget the salt'. Focus on what you want to remember, focus on remembering the salt!

Focus on the positive things you want to do in your cooking adventures. In this way you help your subconscious mind to work with you and, in turn, help you.

Make a move - examine the things you tell yourself today. Rephrase any negative chatter about what you don't want to do, into positive chatter focussed on what you do want to do.

Counting Yourself In: Choosing habits that work

Your habits, like your thoughts and your chatter, either help you or hinder you. Habits work with you for your success or habits pull you away from your success. The habits that you develop around how you respond to challenges will either make your life easier or harder. As an example of a habit let's look at the habits you develop around the kinds of questions you ask in the face of a challenge. Your habits will determine if the challenge is to be a road block or an open door to new solutions.

Let me tell a story of an adventure with a Persimmon Pudding that seemed too small to serve its purpose. I was co-hosting an event for Stanford students and the pudding was to be dessert. Offering to help serve, I was told the challenge; the pudding was large enough for about twelve reasonable portions and there were twice that many guests. And, as this was a very special pudding, everyone would want a taste. What habit of response works well in the face of a challenge?

What if I asked:

"Why are so many people here for dessert?"
"Why is my pudding so small?"
"Why is my whole life falling apart?"

Have you noticed that these questions would quickly lead to remarkable despair. Despair is perhaps an exaggeration, but the direction is definitely down!

Asking, "How?" is a useful proactive habit, it provides you the choices and the opportunity to gain a new perspective and find a creative solution.

Answering the question, "Why have other people caused a problem for me?" (by being here for dessert) leads downhill and to inaction.

Answering the question, "How can I use what I have here?" leads up and into engagement, activity, and a solution.

And with the Persimmon Pudding challenge, here is the question that brought the solution:
"How can I work with the little pudding and make what is needed?"

... keep reading and you'll find out!

Make a move - develop a habit of asking
"How can I solve this?"

Stepping on to choose what you want

Now that you have moved into some more powerful ways to choose to choose, you are ready **to choose what you want**.

A goal to aim for gives you immediate direction. The goal you choose will be affected by the things you value and your own dreams for any moment. Setting your goal in line with the things truly important to you, strengthens you to succeed.

Counting Yourself In: Identifying your values

First take a look at your values; the things that are important to you. Your values will be different from the values of someone else. I, for example, value eating with a crowd of people and being able to include any new folk who show up. My feasts tend to be around relaxed adventures, giving generously, and making new friends. My values here can be listed as adventure, generosity, and friendship.

One way to work out your values around feasting is to think about three occasions when a meal was particularly special and pull out the elements that made those moments precious for you.

Make a move - write down your three key values around eating and feasting.

Counting Yourself In: Identifying your dreams

Your big dreams around your cooking and eating adventures will be your own too. I remember asking myself what my dream feast would be when I found our house in California full of people who we had invited back after an expedition. Hot coffee had sounded great and been accepted and then, as the fun continued, the crowd became hungry. As I had been out of the country for awhile the food supplies in my home were limited.

My ideal dream feast here was something everyone could share. What would feed the crowd?

A few minutes later, with the hungry friends and having only found a large bag of potatoes I was still looking for a solution as to what to eat. I knew I wanted a meal promoting a relaxed and generous atmosphere with unexpected depths of friendship developing all around as people freely laughed and ate. How could I make that happen with only potatoes?

Make a move - draw a picture of a special feast that you want to create. Make the image even more powerful for yourself by using coloured pens.

Counting Yourself In: Identifying your goals

Your goal is what you really want. What goals do you want in line with your values and dreams? Faced with the hungry crowd drinking coffee in my house I thought about the kinds of goals I could set for the feast. What would enable me to give the kind of feast I wanted to give? What would take me towards providing a super supper with an ambience of fun and space for forging strong bonds of friendship?

My eyes fell on a newspaper - in fact a copy of The London Times (I had just returned to California after a visit to family in the UK). And there was an answer to what and how - chips in newspaper just like a British Fish & Chip Shop!

My goal, to have all the potatoes chopped into chips ready to fry in 15 minutes - with a little help from new friends of course!

Make a move - set a goal and then do one thing today to take you nearer to your goal.

Stepping in to make your choice happen

Now you have moved into choosing what you want, the next step is to make your choice happen. Going after what you want is about using 'can do' confidence, helpful beliefs about yourself, and 'will do' motivation.

Counting Yourself In: Working with confidence

There are places in life where you feel confident. These will be different for you than for other people. For you, it might be when you are buying the groceries. Whatever it is, take your thoughts there. Think about how you typically stand, how you typically feel, and what you are typically thinking to yourself and saying to yourself in these confident moments. Bring all these thoughts, feelings and images back to mind in your cooking moments when you are looking for more confidence.

> Make a move - take time to think about yourself in a place where you are very confident. Act out those thoughts, words, and feelings to yourself and remember to act the same way when you want more confidence in a new task.

Counting Yourself In: Working with helpful beliefs

Just like putting on more confidence in challenging situations, you can put on some helpful beliefs about yourself. If you want some ideas, start with this one:

If you know you are the best cook for this feast, what would you be seeing, hearing, and feeling on your cooking adventure?

> Make a move - write down this helpful belief. Remember as you are writing this down you are making it yours so replace the 'you' with 'I'. Then add another helpful belief to the first, and tomorrow, add one more!

Counting Yourself In: Working with motivation

Motivation is about movement (with its roots in the Latin - to move). Movement is necessary to make things happen. You have the power to choose to move to create something remarkable. As you think about something you want to make happen, help yourself get moving by asking the following questions:

Go through the questions fairly rapidly, jotting down an answer for each. Though an unusual combination of questions, it is a powerful sequence.

"What would happen
if you did count yourself in?"

"What would happen
if you didn't count yourself in?"

"What wouldn't happen
if you did count yourself in?"

"What wouldn't happen
if you didn't count yourself in?"

Let's go back to the example of the Persimmon Pudding and the bag of potatoes. In each case:

If I did count myself in,
I would get the feast I wanted.

If I didn't count myself in,
I would see my friends hungry.

If I did count myself in,
I wouldn't get to sit and relax.

If I didn't count myself in,
I wouldn't get the feast I wanted,
and all that I wanted from that feast.

Make a move - think about what it will cost you to Count Yourself In and do the thing you want to do. And then think about what benefits it will give you to Count Yourself In. Use your answers to help you to choose to move on what you want!

Here are the endings to those two challenges I mentioned earlier.

The feast of the Persimmon Pudding

The answer came as I looked across the room and my eyes fell on a plate of oranges. Swiftly I cut them up in attractive slices and lay these across ⅔ of each plate and placed a delicately thin slice of Persimmon Pudding across the other ⅓. There was dessert for everyone. The dessert had a celebratory sparkle as it was passed around and the guests without exception said, "Wow, this looks great! Thank You!" A remarkable success!

The feast of the Super Supper

The answer was, "Chips like the Brits!" I took the potatoes, chipped them, fried them in oil and put portions in newspaper with salt and vinegar! In a jovial atmosphere of salty fingers, happy grins, and relaxed conversation, new friendships were forming. Around the room I heard, "Wow, this is so much fun! Thank You!" A remarkable success!

Let's Eat!

Equipping

Food you may want

Most foods are replaceable in any of the adventures found in this book. This list is one place to start.

Useful for making savoury eats

Onions and garlic
Tomatoes and vegetables of all kinds
Meat, eggs, cheese
Rice, potatoes, pasta
Bread flour, self raising flour, plain flour
Milk, butter/cooking oil
Worcester sauce, soy sauce
Salt and pepper
Herbs and spices - oregano, basil, cinnamon, turmeric, chilli, curry, ginger, paprika
Cans of tomatoes, sweetcorn, beans

Useful for making sweet eats

Butter
Sugar/honey
Fruit, nuts, chocolate, cocoa powder
Cans of peaches, apricots, pineapple

Cups and spoons you may want

For simplicity the measurements are in cupfuls and spoonfuls. Inexpensive sets of measuring cups and spoons are found in most places selling cooking utensils.

A measuring cup holds approximately 250 ml or 8 fl oz. It may help you to know:
Butter, 1 cup is around one 250g packet or 8oz
Flour, 1 cup is around 150g or 5oz
Sugar, 1 cup is around 250g or 8oz

Note: 1 cup is not 250g/8oz for everything. Concentrate now... 50g of sugar weighs the same as 50g of flour (or 50g of anything else for that matter!) but 1 cup of sugar does not weigh the same as 1 cup of flour. Per unit volume, sugar is heavier.

The measuring TABLESPOONS used are a similar size to the spoons usually used to eat cereal, about the size of 4 teaspoons. The teaspoon is a similar size to the spoons usually used to stir coffee.

The Cooking Catalysts in this book do not require precise measurements and assume that the recipes you develop from them will likewise tolerate some inexactness!

Oven temperatures you may want

These oven temperatures are referred to:

Hot oven: 220°C or 425°F or Gas 7

Medium oven: 180°C or 350°F or Gas 4

Cool oven: 140°C or 275°F or Gas 1

Put the oven on for 5-10 minutes before you want to use it, to allow it to heat up.

Baking pans you may want

Begin with the pans you have, checking first that they fit in the oven you are using! Where pan sizes are given it is to provide you with an idea of quantity. Most reasonable pan sizes will work, play around to get the results you want:

For cakes, fill ⅔ pan, expect cake to rise

For bread, expect dough to double in size

For casseroles, expect hot liquid to bubble and rise

For cookies, expect cookies to spread a little

When a greased pan is called for, wipe on just a little oil/butter. Adding a dusting of flour over the oil helps cakes come out of the pans more easily.

Expecting the unexpected

Expect everything, I always say,
and the unexpected never happens.
The Whetherman[2]

Unexpected folk looking for the feast
All the Cooking Catalysts make space for the arrival of a small crowd, invited or otherwise.

If the amount in the pot looks small against the size of the crowd either add some extra canned vegetables into the pot or take time to serve out a portion onto each plate to ensure everyone gets something.   If you still want more food on each plate then add one or more of the following:

Slices of bread cut diagonally or rolls
Slices of fresh fruit
Little mounds of dried fruit, e.g. raisins
Slices of cheese
Salad spread across the plate
And/or...

---

2 Norton Juster, The Phantom Tollbooth, Collins, 1999, ch2/p18

Unexpected feast looking for a name

Be bold in presenting your feast especially if it did not turn out as you planned. Someone, somewhere, probably eats something like this so take courage and name the feast with a flourish. Try using your own name. So I might present my eats as:

Lesley's Extra Hot Chilli Feast
(Perhaps hotter than I had planned!)
or
Lesley's Feast of Chocolate Crisp Cookies
(Perhaps baked for longer than I had planned!)

You get the idea! Be sure to record your surprise results, you may be asked for them again!

Cooking Catalysts

So now, with your Cooking Catalysts to guide you, you can begin your new adventures in creating feasts. Adventures in which,

whilst respecting some universal principles...

like gravity - so,
if you drop an egg then it falls to the floor
unless you catch it!

...you make the choices

Ready to cook your way into your own choices by
playing around with the Cooking Catalysts

Ready for creating your own feasts out of
Your adventures with
Your edibles in
Your kitchen

Ready to seize the choice that is yours
to use what you've got
to get what you want

Get up, Get on and Count Yourself In

This Choice is Yours!

Count Yourself In...

Staff of Life

Here you'll find breads, buns, and batters which include pizza and pancakes!

Among the Cooking Catalysts here you'll learn that Lammas Daily Bread is a useful beginning for lots of kinds of bread and with a little alteration for buns too. It takes a little over 5 minutes to mix and knead dough and then it is set aside to rise. An hour or so later it takes another 5 minutes to make into rolls or loaves. After the dough rises again it takes 15 minutes to cook small rolls and 30 minutes to cook loaves. And I'll show you how to hurry the whole process so that in about an hour you can go from thinking about a hot loaf to eating one.

Be creative in your choices, bold on your adventures, and welcoming of all the unexpected moments that present themselves in all kinds of unexpected ways!

Set yourself free to create **Your Own** eats!

A note on flour
Bread can be made from a variety of flours with a variety of results. Try combinations of white, brown, or seeded bread flour. Different kinds of flours are available in different places. Bread flour has a higher gluten content than cake flour which makes bread flour a good choice for bread. American all purpose flour is something between bread flour and cake flour - for all purposes! Cake flour can be used for bread. In this case the bread will be more cake-like. Experiment with what you have and have fun!

A note on yeast
Warm water for yeast is the correct temperature if made with ⅓ boiling and ⅔ cold water. Yeast does not survive hot temperatures.
Use yeast that can be put directly into flour, (quick yeast, easy bake yeast, rapid rise yeast).

A note on oil/fat
Bread can be baked with no oil/butter but it is the oil/butter that keeps the bread fresher longer. Use the cooking oil you prefer.

A note on salt
Remember the salt. It gives the bread flavour. If you often leave salt out of things you may still want to keep the salt in your bread.

A note on kneading

Kneading bread - Once the liquid is mixed in then begin to push, stretch, and fold the dough over and over using the heel of your hand. If you are using a large bowl this can be done in the bowl. After 5-10 minutes the dough will spring back when pushed and is ready to be left to rise.

A note on rising dough

Bread likes a warm place to rise. The time it takes to rise and how much it rises depends on many factors. Plan for an hour for each rise. Cover with a cloth and be patient!

A note on making bread in an hour

When time is short, make loaves, put loaves on baking pans, and put these baking pans directly into a cold oven. Turn the oven on and give the loaves an extra 15 minutes cooking in the oven. (Yeast will continue to work for awhile as oven warms and so loaves will grow). Bread made fast is still tasty.

A note on shaping bread

You can shape your loaves as you want. And pushing the dough around while you decide on a shape is OK too. Dough likes handling. If you make loaves of fairly similar sizes they will take the same length of time to cook.

You can make round loaves or oblong loaves on baking sheets, or loaves the shape of any baking pan you have. You can have fun playing around with the dough and make all kinds of interesting shapes.

To make braids
Take dough for one loaf. Divide into 3 and make 3 ropes of dough. Attach the ropes together at one end and then braid.

To make cottage loaves
Take ⅔ of dough for one loaf and make into a round. Take the ⅓ left and make a smaller round. Put smaller round on top of larger round and secure the two pieces together at the centre by pushing your finger all the way through both pieces.

To make knots
Take dough for one loaf. Roll into a rope and simply tie this rope in a knot.

These shapes can also be made as rolls.

Lammas Daily Bread

Gather up

- ✓ Bread flour, 10 cups (one 1.5kg/3lb bag)
- ✓ Yeast, 3 teaspoons,
- ✓ Sugar, 3 teaspoons
- ✓ Salt, 3 teaspoons
- ✓ Oil/melted butter, 3 TABLESPOONS
- ✓ Warm water, 3¾ cups (850 ml/30 fl oz)

Go for it

- ➡ Mix dry ingredients together in a large bowl
- ➡ Stir in oil/melted butter
- ➡ Add warm water
- ➡ Knead 5 minutes in bowl until dough is springy
- ➡ Leave dough in bowl to rise and double in size (this first rising can be skipped if you are rushed)
- ➡ Punch down dough to release air after rising
- ➡ Knead lightly again in bowl
- ➡ Divide into 3 or 4 loaves, or 36 rolls
- ➡ Put on greased baking sheets or bread pans
- ➡ Rise bread again until double in size
- ➡ Cook in hot oven for 30 minutes for loaves, 15-20 minutes for rolls

Chat

-If bread is cooked it should sound hollow when bottom base is tapped. Put bread on a cooling rack to allow the moisture to evaporate while it cools.

Pizza

This has a bread dough base so begin with the Lammas Daily Bread dough. (Makes 6 large pizzas)

Gather up

✓ Bread dough that has risen once
✓ Tomatoes, 2-3 cups (chopped or pureed)
✓ Basil or oregano or both
✓ Cheese, 1-2 cups grated cheese for each pizza
✓ Grated or chopped onion
✓ Cooked meat/fruit/vegetables for toppings

Go for it

Dough

➡ Punch down the risen dough and knead a little
➡ Divide dough into number of pizzas you want
➡ Roll out and stretch dough onto greased pans
➡ Leave dough to rise again, 30-60 minutes
➡ Prick dough with fork, cook in hot oven for about 10 minutes until dough is light brown
➡ Remove pizza bases from oven

Topping

➡ Spread tomatoes on pizza base, sprinkle on herbs
➡ Grate cheese and sprinkle over tomatoes
➡ Chop onion finely and sprinkle over cheese
➡ Top with cooked meat/fruit/vegetables of choice
➡ Put pizzas back into hot oven for 20-30 minutes until crust is brown and cheese melted

Chat

-Any cheese that melts is fine, e.g mozzarella, feta, or cheddar. 125g/4 oz cheese will make about 1½ cups of grated cheese.

-Before rising, the dough can be frozen in pizza size pieces. When required take out of freezer in the morning, put in a bowl, cover with cloth and leave in a warm place. By evening the dough will have thawed and risen.

-Any tomatoes will work; you can use fresh chopped tomatoes, canned chopped tomatoes, pureed tomatoes, or passata.

Cinnamon Rolls

Gather up

- √ Bread flour, 10 cups
- √ Yeast, 3 teaspoons
- √ Sugar, 6 TABLESPOONS
- √ Salt, 3 teaspoons
- √ Oil/butter, 3 TABLESPOONS
- √ Eggs, 3,
- √ Warm milk, 1½ cups
- √ Warm water, 1½ cups
- √ Butter, cinnamon, dried fruit, sugar, nuts, for filling

Go for it

- ➡ Mix dry ingredients together in a large bowl
- ➡ Stir in oil/melted butter
- ➡ Mix eggs, milk and water, and stir into flour
- ➡ Knead until dough springs back, divide into three

- ➡ Roll out each piece of dough into a rectangle (about 45cm/18 inches x 30cm/12 inches)
- ➡ Spread dough with butter, cinnamon, dried fruit, sugar, nuts, or any filling you want in your buns
- ➡ Roll up to make a long sausage
- ➡ Cut into 12 slices for 12 buns
- ➡ Place buns onto greased pans
- ➡ Leave to rise until double in size

- ➡ Cook in medium oven for 30 minutes

Icing to make while Cinnamon Rolls are cooking

Gather up

√ Icing sugar, 2 cups
√ Vanilla (or flavouring of choice), 2 teaspoons
√ Warm water, 2 TABLESPOONS

Go for it

➡ Add water to icing sugar a little at a time
➡ Mix in flavouring
➡ Drizzle a little icing onto each hot bun

Chat

-The dough for Cinnamon Rolls is very similar to Lammas Daily Bread, made richer and softer by replacing part of the water with milk and eggs. The dough is also made sweeter by adding more sugar.

-When kneading and working with dough, add more liquid if the dough is not sticking together or add more flour if it is too sticky. Just get the dough together, get it off your fingers and get it into the oven!

-If you are wondering which way to roll up the rectangle, the answer is - this choice is yours! One way gives you wider flatter buns and the other way gives you taller buns. You figure out what you want! And incidentally, you can put the buns down any way you want on the baking pans. Experiment!

-If you want a thicker icing, add more icing sugar.

Iced Buns

These have a Cinnamon Roll dough base. For Iced Buns you do not need to roll out the dough

Go for it

➡ Divide dough into

Either

24 pieces to make sausage shapes for finger buns

Or

28 pieces to make into 4 large bun rounds. For each bun round, put 1 bun in the middle and 6 buns around it. Small buns join up as they rise and swell

➡ Put buns onto greased baking sheets
➡ Let buns rise until double in size
➡ Cook in medium oven, for 20 minutes (a little longer for bun rounds) until buns are light brown
➡ Put icing on buns when the buns are cold

Icing

➡ Make as for Cinnamon Rolls
➡ For pink icing add a drop of red food colouring

Variation

➡ <u>Hot Cross Buns:</u> Add some dried fruit and mixed spice (2-3 teaspoons), shape into round buns, cut a cross on the top of each and cook as iced buns

Dave's 'enough for a crowd' Yorkshire Pudding

The great British favourite to eat hot with beef

Gather up

- ✓ Flour, 2½ cups
- ✓ Eggs, 4
- ✓ Milk, 1½ cups
- ✓ Water, 1 cup
- ✓ Salt to taste
- ✓ Oil for pan, 2 TABLESPOONS

Go for it

- ➡ Put oil into a large pan
- ➡ Put pan into a hot oven to heat oil
- ➡ Put flour and salt in a large bowl
- ➡ Gradually mix egg, milk, and water into flour
- ➡ Once oil is hot, remove pan from oven and add batter which should sizzle in the oil
- ➡ Cook Yorkshire in oven for about 30 minutes

Chat

–Pan size is approximately 5cm/2 inches deep and 38cm/15 inches by 25cm/10 inches.

–To check oil is hot enough test with a spoonful of batter. If no sizzle when batter hits the oil then return pan to oven to continue heating up the oil.

–Using pan that roasted meat has been taken from works well. Yorkshire can cook in meat fat.

–For small Yorkshires, make ¼ amount, put a little hot oil in 12 muffin tins, add batter, cook 15 minutes.

Lammas Sunday Pancakes

Makes 50-60 pancakes

Gather up

✓ Butter, 1 cup
✓ Self raising flour, 6½ cups
✓ Sugar, ½ cup
✓ Eggs, 6
✓ Milk, 6 cups

Go for it

➡ Melt butter
➡ Mix dry ingredients together in a large bowl
➡ In another bowl, mix eggs and milk together
➡ Add melted butter to eggs and milk
➡ Add wet ingredients to dry ingredients
➡ Stir until just combined

➡ Put a little oil on a griddle or heavy frying pan
➡ Heat griddle
➡ Drop batter in large spoonfuls onto hot griddle. Batter should sizzle as it touches the pan
➡ Cook for 1 or 2 minutes until the upper surfaces of the pancake look bubbly and dry
➡ Lift edges of pancakes and if the bottom looks smooth and golden then flip. Cook for about half the time on the second side
➡ Remove from griddle and keep warm in low oven
➡ Replenish oil on griddle as necessary

Pancake variations

➡ <u>Oat pancakes:</u> Replace 1 cup of flour with 2 cups of oats

➡ <u>Fruit pancakes:</u> Drop dried or fresh fruit onto pancakes before flipping

➡ <u>Savoury pancakes:</u> Leave out sugar and use as a base for a savoury topping

➡ <u>Your pancakes:</u> ...

Chat

-If there is yoghurt or cream you want to use, this can replace some or all of the milk.

-If you are a bit short of milk then some of the milk can be replaced with water.

-Turn down heat if pancakes are cooking fast on the outside without cooking in the middle.

-Can replace butter with oil.

Welsh Pikelets - similar to drop scones
Makes 15-20 pikelets

Gather up
✓ Self raising flour, 1½ cups
✓ Sugar, ¼ cup
✓ Eggs, 2
✓ Milk, 1¼ cups

Go for it
➡ Mix dry ingredients together in a large bowl
➡ Add wet ingredients to dry ingredients and mix
➡ Put a little oil on a griddle or heavy frying pan
➡ Heat griddle
➡ Drop batter in large spoonfuls onto hot griddle
➡ When bubbles rise on surface, flip pikelet
➡ Cook until golden on both sides
➡ Replenish oil on griddle as necessary

Chat
-Usually a little smaller than American breakfast pancakes and when I was a child these were a treat made with my Mamgu (Grandmother) in Wales. We ate them cold with jam and butter. Later I realised pikelets are very similar to the breakfast pancakes which are eaten hot with maple syrup and often contain lots of butter.
-When I was a child, as these cakes came off the griddle they were put between cloths to keep in the steam as they cooled, it keeps the pikelets moist.

Scones

Gather up
✓ Self raising flour, 4 cups
✓ Milk, 2 cups
✓ Sugar, 1-2 TABLESPOONS

Go for it
➡ Stir sugar into flour
➡ Add milk
➡ Knead mixture gently to a soft dough

➡ For large scone rounds: Make dough into two large balls. Press each down gently with your hand until about 3-4cm/1½ inches thick. Cut into 8 wedges and keep together for cooking as one round

➡ For small scones: Shape into 24 balls and flatten slightly or if you prefer, roll out dough on a floured board to 3cm/1¼ inches thick and cut out with a cutter

➡ Cook on greased baking sheets in hot oven:
     -for scone rounds - 20-30 minutes
     -for small scones - 12-15 minutes

➡ Eat as fresh as possible

Scone variations

➡ <u>Fruit scones:</u> Add 1 TABLESPOON extra sugar, 2 TABLESPOONS dried fruit, and 1 teaspoon of cinnamon/mixed spice

➡ <u>Whole wheat scones:</u> Replace half white flour with self raising whole wheat flour and replace some milk with a beaten egg

➡ <u>Your favourite scones:</u> Add up to ¼ cup of whatever dry ingredients you want - dates, walnuts, chocolate pieces - your choice

➡ <u>Crumbly, buttery scones:</u> Replace ½ cup of the milk with ½ cup butter, rub butter into flour, then stir in sugar and add milk, knead and shape

Chat

-For a long time I had issues with the height of my scones; I wanted them taller but was unsure how to encourage them to rise more in the oven. One day however, I had an ahha moment and realised that to get them to come out of the oven as taller scones I needed to put them into the oven as taller scones; make them thicker!

Oatmeal Porridge Breakfast

Gather up

For each person:

✓ Oats, ⅓ cup

✓ Milk or water, ⅔ cup

Go for it

➡ Put oats and milk or water into saucepan

➡ Heat gently, stirring from time to time

➡ When porridge is thick, remove from heat

➡ Eat as it is or top with:

      -Butter and honey

      -Cream and sugar

      -Syrup

      -Fruit

      -Anything you like!

Chat

-Two things are well known about breakfast:

      -Breakfast is a very important meal

      -Breakfast is the most often skipped meal

Soups, Salads, Suppers and Sizzles

Introductory comments

Here you'll find cool salads and hot curries and how to make your own spicy oven fries.

Among the Cooking Catalysts here you'll learn what makes the soup different from the curry (more liquid in the soup of course). And how to make a curry in a hurry or a chilli. And how vegetables, meat, or both, or something else, can be put with rice or pasta or potato to make a supper for yourself. And I'll show you how to put a hot home made soup on the table in less than half an hour.

Be creative in your choices, bold on your adventures and welcoming of all the unexpected moments that present themselves in all kinds of unexpected ways!

Set yourself free to create **Your Own** eats!

A note on cutting meat and vegetables

Meat and vegetables can be cut into any shape or size for the soups and casseroles. As you cut, remember the larger the pieces the longer your dish will take to cook and that some food like soup is easier to eat if the pieces in it fit into your mouth.

A note on garnishes

Dishes of food can be garnished with leaves of mint, coriander, parsley, or anything edible. If the garnish is to go on soup it needs to be light enough to float!

A note on using stock or bouillon cubes

Stock cubes or bouillon cubes add flavour to dishes. Remember they contain salt so taste your cooking before adding more salt. Another way of adding flavour is to add a little more salt and pepper, or gradually add some of your favourite herbs or spice.

A note on chopping an onion
Begin by chopping onion in half lengthwise. Next place cut side on board and cut right into it both ways as if you were drawing lines of latitude and longitude and you should end up with small pieces. Any safe method for obtaining small pieces will do.

A note on frying
Put a spoonful of oil into the pan you are using (or knob of butter but if using butter heat very gently) and heat for a minute or two. When frying onions, move onions around in the pan until they turn clear.

A note on garlic
Garlic can be added to most savoury dishes. Peel off outside layer and push clove of garlic through a garlic press or just chop very finely. Garlic is pungent and its smell lingers on things with which it comes in contact.

Go for it

Croutons
➡ Fry up small cubes of bread (stale will do) in a little oil or butter (with herbs and spices if you want) until crispy
➡ Add to soup or salad just before serving

Garlic bread
➡ Slice a baguette lengthwise
➡ Butter generously
➡ Sprinkle with fresh garlic or dried garlic
➡ Shut loaf pieces together
➡ Wrap in foil
➡ Heat in hot oven for 20 minutes

Herb or cheese bread
➡ Make as garlic bread but without garlic
➡ Sprinkle herbs and spices or a little grated cheese on the buttered baguette before putting it into the oven

Chat
-Any bread (including stale bread) can be put in a hot oven for a few minutes to crisp up. It can be buttered first if you prefer.

Leek and Potato Soup or Soup Base

Gather up

✓ Oil/butter for frying, 1-2 TABLESPOONS

For each person:

✓ Leek, ½ cup

✓ Potato, ½ cup

✓ Water, ¾ cup

✓ Salt/pepper/herbs/spices to season to your taste

Go for it

➡ Trim top and bottom off each leek

➡ Discard these end pieces and outer leaves

➡ Slice up the rest of the leek, wash thoroughly

➡ Peel and chop potato

➡ Fry the leek in a saucepan with oil/butter

➡ Add herbs and spices to taste

➡ Add potato and water and bring to the boil

➡ Boil gently for 20-30 minutes until potato is cooked

➡ With a blender, make soup into a smooth, thick broth

Chat

-This is a great soup as it is, and also a good base for most other soups. Onions or spring onions can be substituted for leeks.

-If this is a soup base, add other vegetables, liquid, herbs and spices as wanted and reduce quantity of leeks and potato for each person.

Vegetable Soup

Gather up

✓ Oil/butter for frying, 1-2 TABLESPOONS

For each person:

✓ Onion, ¼ cup

✓ Vegetables, ¾ cup

✓ Water, ¾ cup

✓ Salt/pepper/herbs/spices to season to your taste

Go for it

➡ Wash and chop vegetables

➡ Chop and fry onion in oil/butter

➡ Add herbs and spices to taste

➡ Add chopped vegetables and water

➡ Boil gently until vegetables are cooked

➡ Allow 20-30 minutes for cooking, depending on size of vegetables and how soft you want them

Chat

-If you chop the vegetables very small, you can cook this soup in 15-20 minutes.

-If you prefer, the soup can be pureed with a blender into a thick even broth. Soup will be thicker if there is potato in it.

-Leftovers are great in soup. Add vegetables 10 minutes before serving as they only need to heat through. Add frozen leftovers from a previous meal at the same time as anything uncooked as these need to defrost and heat through.

Chicken or Ham Bone Soup

Gather up

✓ Chicken or ham bones
For each person:
✓ Onion, chopped, ¼ cup
✓ Vegetables, chopped, ½ cup
✓ Water, to cover bones in saucepan
✓ Noodles, rice or potato, ½ cup cooked

Go for it

➡ Put chicken or ham bone leftovers in saucepan and cover with water
➡ Boil until meat is falling off the bones adding more water as necessary
➡ Take bones out of water and remove any meat still on bones. Discard bones
➡ Ensure the meat does not contain any small bone pieces and return meat to water
➡ Add onion, vegetables, and noodles and continue heating until everything is cooked

Chat

–If you decide to add uncooked rice or noodles you will probably only want up to ¼ cup for each person as rice and noodles swell in cooking, taking up some of the water. Keep an eye on the amount of liquid in the pot adding more if needed.
–The bones enrich the soup even with little meat.

Corn Chowder

Gather up

✓ Oil/butter for frying, 1 TABLESPOON

For each person:

✓ Onion, ¼ cup

✓ Milk, 1 cup

✓ Sweetcorn, ¼ cup

✓ Potato, ½ cup

✓ Salt/pepper/herbs/spices to season to your taste

Go for it

➡ Peel and chop potato

➡ Chop and fry onion in oil/butter

➡ Add potato with milk and sweetcorn

➡ Cook soup gently until potato is soft

Chat

-Traditionally a chowder contained fish of some kind. Today it is often used to refer to any thick creamy soup containing potato, onions, milk, or cream.

-For this soup, some milk can be replaced with water.

-The sweetcorn measure is particularly flexible. If you are using canned sweetcorn, adding one small or medium can usually works for most quantities of soup.

Lettuce Based Salads

Go for it

➡ This is the familiar salad. Wash and chop lettuce, with tomatoes and cucumber, and anything else you want to put in

➡ Mix together

➡ Toss with a salad dressing just before serving or offer a salad dressing separately

➡ Serve in individual bowls or leave in a large bowl

Chat

-Simple salads are made by chopping up various salad ingredients in various ways and mixing them in various combinations to make your choice salad.

-If you want avocado in your salad then prepare and add into salad just before eating to retain avocado's fresh, green colour.

-Grapes work well in a salad with lettuce.

Salad Dressings

To ensure salad stays crispy toss just before serving

Go for it - Oil and vinegar dressing

➡ Mix 1 cup vinegar, ⅔ cup oil, and ⅓ cup water
➡ Add garlic and spices to taste. Try Worcester sauce, soy sauce, salt, pepper, mustard, and garlic

Go for it - Thousand island dressing

➡ Take ½ cup ketchup
➡ Add enough mayonnaise to turn ketchup pink
➡ Add enough dill pickle or lemon juice or something like tabasco to sharpen the flavour

Go for it - Your own salad dressing

➡ Start with oil and vinegar and ...
➡ Or start with mayonnaise and ...
➡ Or start with natural yoghurt and play around with different flavours - honey, ginger, curry, chilli

Chat

−If you choose to use olive oil as the oil in your salad dressing then keep olive oil clear by storing salad dressing out of the refrigerator. Experiment with different kinds of oil and different kinds of vinegar for an assortment of tastes.

Fruit and Nut Based Salads / Waldorf

Gather up
✓ Apple
✓ Raisins
✓ Celery
✓ Walnuts
✓ Lemon juice
✓ Mayonnaise to taste

Go for it
➡ Chop, mix, taste, adjust, mix again, taste
➡ When satisfied with mix, eat

Fruit and nut salad variations
➡ Mix of any fresh fruit chopped as you want
➡ Mix of raisin and carrot and pineapple
➡ Mix of dried fruit and nuts and coconut

Chat
-Keeps 2-3 days in refrigerator.

Vegetable Based Salads / Coleslaw

Gather up
✓ White cabbage
✓ Carrots, roughly same volume as cabbage
✓ Onion to taste
✓ Mayonnaise to taste

Go for it
➡ Shred or grate cabbage
➡ Shred or grate carrots
➡ Chop onion into very small pieces
➡ Mix everything with some mayonnaise

➡ Try some substitutions!

Vegetable salad variations
➡ Add orange pieces
➡ Add nuts and grapes
➡ Add seeds such as pumpkin, sesame, or sunflower

Chat
-Keeps 2-3 days in refrigerator.

Cooked Vegetables

Vegetables can take the place of meat in most dishes. Here are some basic notes on cooking vegetables. Timings are a guide, cook the vegetables until they are as soft as you want them. Add the herbs and spices you want with salt and pepper.

Go for it - Pan fry vegetables

➡ Put 1-2 TABLESPOONS oil/butter in a frying pan,
➡ Add vegetables, fry for 5-10 minutes

Go for it - Oven roast vegetables

➡ Put vegetables in an ovenproof dish
➡ Add some oil/butter, garlic, and a little water
➡ Cook 30-45 minutes in medium oven
➡ Stir from time to time
➡ For less crispy vegetables, cover with lid or foil

Go for it - Steamed vegetables

➡ Put vegetables in a steamer above a pan of boiling water and cook 5 minutes. (Retains colour and flavour of green leafy vegetables)

Go for it - Boiled vegetables

➡ Put vegetables in a saucepan with boiling water, boil gently for 15-20 minutes

Go for it - Raw vegetables

➡ Many vegetables can be eaten without cooking

Pasta

Gather up

For each person:

√ 1½ cups uncooked pasta (100g/2 oz)

Go for it

➡ Put pasta into boiling water, add salt and cook. It says on packet how much and how long, usually 10-12 minutes

➡ Once cooked and drained, a little oil and pepper tossed into the pasta keeps individual pieces separate and adds a little flavour

➡ Grated cheese is popular with pasta, either on top of another topping or by itself on top or stirred in

Chat

-About boiling water. I was once asked how you can tell when water is boiling ready for the pasta. To my surprise this question came from a 19 year old who had just achieved 100% on an A-level physics module. I replied, "When it bubbles", and he then asked about the size of the bubbles. So just to clarify for any other physicists out there - the answer is that for pasta we want vigorously boiling water - big bubbles!

Pasta Toppings and Stir-ins

Go for it
Choose one!
- ➡ Fry small pieces of ham and mushroom and add to cooked pasta with cream cheese
- ➡ Fry small pieces of bacon and add to cooked pasta with uncooked spinach and cream or milk
- ➡ Melt some grated cheese into a pan of slowly heating milk and add to cooked pasta
- ➡ Melt some grated cheese into a white sauce and add to cooked pasta (see lasagne - white sauce)
- ➡ Fry some chopped vegetables in butter and garlic and stir into cooked pasta
- ➡ Fry some chopped spring onion, add tomatoes and sweetcorn and stir into cooked pasta
- ➡ Add anything you want into cooked pasta!

Chat
-Cut all vegetables small enough to cook quickly when fried in a pan.

-The great thing about stir-ins is they work well even if there is little to stir-in! So if lots of extra folk show up before you cook the pasta, just add more pasta and perhaps add a can of tomatoes, or something else into the stir-in.

Lasagne

This dish has 3 different kinds of layers and grated cheese on top.
Pan size, 23cm/9 inches by 30cm/12 inches

Gather up - Lasagne noodles
✓ Approximately 12-15 Lasagne noodles

Gather up - Tomato based sauce
✓ Oil, 2 TABLESPOONS
✓ Onion, 1
✓ Minced/ground beef, vegetables or both, 2-3 cups
✓ Tomatoes (chopped, pureed or sieved), 2 cups
✓ Salt, pepper, oregano to taste

Go for it
➡ Chop onion and fry in oil
➡ Add any meat and fry until brown
➡ Add vegetables, tomatoes, salt, pepper and herbs
➡ Cover, add a little water if necessary and simmer until meat and vegetables are cooked, 20 minutes

Variation
➡ Spinach lasagne: Replace meat and some or all of the vegetables with finely chopped spinach

Gather up - White sauce

✓ Milk, 3 cups
✓ Butter, 3 TABLESPOONS
✓ Flour, 3 TABLESPOONS

Go for it

➡ Melt butter in saucepan
➡ Stir in flour and cook gently for 1 minute
➡ Remove pan from heat
➡ Add milk gradually, stirring constantly
➡ Return to heat and simmer for 5 minutes stirring all the time

Go for it - Putting it all together

➡ Grease the dish and then add in this order:
➡ 1. lasagne, 2. tomato layer, 3. white sauce,
   4. lasagne, 5. tomato layer, 6. white sauce,
   7. lasagne, 8. white sauce, 9. grated cheese
➡ Cook in hot oven for 30 minutes

Chat

-When making the white sauce, add the milk very gradually to keep sauce smooth. The sauce thickens as the flour cooks. Use electric whisk to smooth if necessary.
-Number of layers is not important, make more layers if your dish is deep.
-Need 1-2cm/¾ inch of space above final layer to keep sauce in the pan while cooking.

Rice

For each person, ½ cup uncooked rice, which will make 1 cup cooked rice

➡ Twice the water to rice so 1 cup of rice with 2 cups of water and a little salt

➡ Cook on stove or in oven or in rice cooker

➡ **Cooking rice on the stove,** put rice and water in a pan, bring water to boil and simmer with lid on. Follow timing on packet. Once rice is cooked all water should be absorbed. Stop cooking at this point or add more water if rice needs more cooking

➡ **Cooking rice in the oven,** put rice in a dish with a lid, pour boiling water onto rice. Cook 30 - 60 minutes depending on type of rice used.   See directions on packet and allow a few minutes extra when cooking rice in the oven

➡ **Using a rice cooker,** put rice and water into cooker and follow instructions for cooker.   Be sure to switch rice cooker on!

Chat

-Cooked rice can be fried in a little oil with a number of things such as meat, vegetables, or eggs. Put meat, vegetables or egg in pan first to be sure they are cooked/reheated through before adding rice.

Curries and Casseroles

Gather up

✓ Oil/butter for frying
✓ Onion
✓ Garlic (optional)
✓ Meat, vegetables or both, 1 cup for each person
✓ Spice for curry
✓ Apples and raisins or other fruit (optional)
✓ Flour, 2 TABLESPOONS
✓ Water to cover everything

Go for it

➡ Chop and fry onion and garlic in oil/butter
➡ Add curry spice experimenting with ¼ teaspoon for each cup of curry
➡ Chop meat into bite size pieces, add to onion, and fry until browned
➡ Stir in flour to thicken
➡ Chop any vegetables, stir in
➡ Add water to cover everything
➡ Add any fresh or dried fruit

Either

➡ Cook on stove top using a medium heat for 20-30 minutes stirring from time to time to ensure even cooking

Or

➡ Transfer to ovenproof dish with lid and cook in medium oven until meat and vegetables are cooked, 1-1½ hours

Chat

-If you make the curry too spicy, add raisins. The sweetness of the fruit takes away some of the spiciness. Alternatively, serve with fruit such as pineapple, or banana, and/or yoghurt.

-Thickening curries and casseroles: Once the onion is fried then a TABLESPOON of flour can be stirred in before adding liquid, or use pieces of potato. It is the starch that thickens the mix.

-For curries and casseroles you need roughly the same volume of liquid as the meat or vegetables.

-You can make up your own curry out of a variety of spices but 'curry powder' which is a blend of spices may serve your purpose in early adventures while you are refining your feasts.

-Cheaper cuts of meat may take longer to cook. Also, cooking with cheaper meat may mean you want to drain off excess fat once meat is cooked and before adding anything else.

Chilli

Gather up

✓ Oil/butter for frying
✓ Onion
✓ Garlic (optional)
✓ Meat, vegetables or both, 1 cup for each person
✓ Chilli powder
✓ Canned red kidney beans
✓ Flour, 2 TABLESPOONS
✓ Tomatoes and water to cover everything

Go for it

➡ Chop and fry onion and garlic in oil/butter
➡ Add chilli powder experimenting with ¼ teaspoon for each cup of chilli
➡ Chop meat, add to onion, and fry until browned
➡ Stir in flour to thicken
➡ Chop any vegetables and stir in
➡ Add canned red kidney beans
➡ Add enough tomatoes to cover everything (and add extra water if wanted)

Either

➡ Continue to simmer on stove top until meat and vegetables are cooked, 20-30 minutes stirring from time to time to ensure even cooking

Or

➡ Transfer to ovenproof dish with lid and cook in medium oven until meat and vegetables are cooked, about 1-1½ hours

Chat

-If you use all vegetables or a combination of vegetables and meat the chilli will be less heavy than a meat only chilli would be.

-If using vegetables that take a long time to cook (swede, turnips, carrots) then either slice thin or cook ahead of time.

-Limit the amount of dark green leafy vegetable like spring greens as they have a strong flavour.

-If using dried red kidney beans research proper cooking method to ensure toxins are destroyed and beans safe to eat. Using canned kidney beans which are already cooked is an easier option!

-Amount of chilli powder will depend on how spicy you want the dish and the strength of your spice.

-If using fresh chilli peppers take care to wash hands thoroughly and avoid contact with the eyes or mouth.

-A popular choice of meat for chilli is minced/ground beef.

Baked Potatoes

Go for it
➡ Scrub potato skins to remove any dirt
➡ Pierce all the potatoes with 3 or 4 holes

Either
➡ Cook in hot oven for 1-1½ hours

Or
➡ Cook in microwave - how long depends on size of potato - try 4-5 minutes per potato (adding 2-3 minutes for each extra potato you put in) and then cook for longer if necessary. If you are only cooking a few potatoes this method is fast. It does not produce such crispy crusty potato skins

Chat
-If you are expecting a large crowd then allow time to prepare potatoes, or choose rice or pasta!!

-Most potatoes need peeling or scrubbing before use.

-If you have a large crowd then using the microwave to cook potatoes may not be quite as fast as you imagine as you need to add extra time per potato. The potatoes will be very hot!

Baked Potato Toppings

Go for it

Cut cooked potato open and top with one of the following:
➡ Butter and grated cheese
➡ Tuna and mayonnaise
➡ Any meat or vegetable topping
➡ Baked beans with grated cheese
➡ Your choice...

Chat

-If using cheese or butter then giving out a fixed size portion with each dinner will reduce the amount of cheese and butter used. Some sort of veggie mix is an inexpensive way to feed a crowd.

-To make a veggie mix, start with frying an onion, add a can of tomatoes, and then be creative with other food you have to hand.

-Left over baked potatoes can be sliced and fried. Add a sprinkle of paprika or chilli powder for something more spicy.

Roast Potatoes or Oven Fries

Gather up
√ Potatoes
√ Spices if wanted
√ Oil for roasting

Go for it - Method one: Boiling and then roasting
➡ Peel and chop potatoes
➡ Boil in a pan of water for 20 minutes
➡ Remove from water and coat in oil
➡ Add spices if you want
➡ Roast the potatoes in hot oven for 30-60 minutes depending on size

Go for it - Method two: Just roasting
➡ Peel and chop potatoes
➡ Pour oil over potatoes in baking tray and swish potatoes around in the oil
➡ Add spices if you want
➡ Roast the potatoes in hot oven for 60-90 minutes depending on size

Chat
–When you cut the potatoes, choose the size and shape, so if you want oven fries then cut potatoes into the oven fry shape and size you want!

Boiled and Mashed Potatoes

Go for it

➡ Peel and chop potatoes
➡ Put in a saucepan of water. Add a little salt if wanted. Using boiling water will speed up the process
➡ Once water is boiling, boil steadily for as long as it takes for potatoes to go soft. Allow 30-45 minutes depending on how small you chopped the potatoes
➡ For mashed potatoes - Drain the potatoes and then add a little milk and butter and then with a potato masher, mash until creamy

Cottage Pie

The potato with it's topping underneath!

Gather up

- √ Oil/butter for frying, 1-2 TABLESPOONS
- √ Onion, 1
- √ Carrots, 2
- √ Flour, 1 TABLESPOON
- √ Stock/bouillon, 1¼ cups
- √ Ketchup, 4 TABLESPOONS
- √ Tomatoes, 2 cups
- √ Dried herbs, ½ teaspoon oregano or basil
- √ Pinch of salt and pepper
- √ Minced/ground beef, 3 or 4 cups
- √ Worcester/soy sauce, 1 TABLESPOON

Go for it

- ➡ Peel, chop, and fry onion and carrots in oil/butter
- ➡ Add meat and fry until cooked
- ➡ Stir in flour and cook for 1 minute
- ➡ Gradually stir in the stock and bring to the boil
- ➡ Add tomato, Worcester/soy sauce, herbs, seasoning and ketchup to taste
- ➡ Simmer 15-20 minutes until carrots are cooked
- ➡ Put this sauce into a large ovenproof dish
- ➡ Put mashed potatoes on top
- ➡ Serve immediately or put in a hot oven to brown the potato for 15-20 minutes

Chat

-Putting finished cottage pie into the oven warms the dish (if the meat and potato is put into a cold dish the dinner will cool quickly).

-Can mix some grated cheese into mashed potatoes for a tasty variety or sprinkle cheese on top.

-Can use stock left over from previously cooking vegetables or make stock with a stock cube or bouillon cube and a mug of boiling water.

-Some or all of the meat in this dish can be replaced with vegetables.

Oven Baked Chicken Pieces with a Sauce

Gather up
✓ Chicken, one piece for each person

Go for it
➡ Put chicken in an ovenproof dish
➡ Cover the chicken with the sauce
➡ Cook in hot oven for 45-60 minutes depending on size of chicken portions
➡ Check on chicken halfway through, and add more liquid if necessary to keep chicken moist

Ideas for quick sauces
➡ Veggie sauce - fry onion, add vegetables, tomatoes and some water. Pour over chicken
➡ Fruity sauce - open a can of fruit in fruit juice such as pineapple, apricots, or prunes, and simply pour the whole lot over the chicken with a little water

Chat
-You may prefer skinless chicken pieces.
-You can brown the chicken by frying it in a little oil before putting into dish with sauce. This is just for appearance as the chicken will not brown in the sauce.

Oven Baked Crispy Chicken Pieces

Gather up
- ✓ Chicken, one piece for each person
- ✓ Butter or oil
- ✓ Spices (optional)
- ✓ Nuts or cornflakes (optional)

Go for it
- ➡ Put melted butter or oil in a bowl
- ➡ Dip chicken in the butter or oil
- ➡ Add spices of your choice if you want
- ➡ Dip the 'sticky with oil or butter' chicken into a bowl of crushed cornflakes or flaked/chopped nuts or crumb coating of choice
- ➡ Put chicken in an ovenproof dish
- ➡ Sprinkle remainder of crumbs over chicken
- ➡ Put in hot oven and cook for 45-60 minutes until chicken is cooked (check the thickest part of the chicken, the meat should be dry and juices clear)

Chat
-Uncooked chicken carries harmful bacteria so be careful to discard any unused butter or oil into which raw chicken has been dipped. Also, discard any unused crumb coating.

Lamb Chops, Pork Chops, Beef Steaks

Go for it

➡ Put meat in a pan of oil and fry until done, turning once. If you have a fabulous beef steak this is one way to do it

➡ Alternatively chops/steak can be covered in sauce of choice or just a little oil and oven baked in a hot oven for 30-60 minutes depending on size. Cut the thickest one in half if you want to check the meat is cooked. Except in the case of beef which can be eaten rare, juices from meat should run clear

➡ Experiment with sauces

Ideas for quick sauces

➡ Combinations of tomatoes/ketchup, stock and strong coffee make for interesting barbecue flavours that work well with pork

➡ Combinations of fried onions and mushrooms with herbs and spices and a little water

Chat

-If you have more people eating than portions of meat, cut the meat into smaller pieces add vegetables and serve. Each person then has a few small portions of meat with vegetables.

Fish

Go for it

➡ Cook in hot oven, wrapped in foil, with butter and slices of lemon or lime

➡ Cook until fish is flaky (approximately 30 minutes depending on size/thickness of fish)

Or

➡ Fry in pan with a little oil/butter - flip fish halfway through cooking

Chat

-With its more delicate flavour, fish is usually spiced more gently.

Marinades

Go for it

➡ A basic marinade is usually oil with something spicy. Start by experimenting with half oil and half soy sauce with some garlic and ginger. You can either put meat in a flat pan or piled up in a bowl. The marinade needs to be put onto the meat or the meat sat in the marinade and turned once in awhile. The flavours in the marinade need to be strong enough to be tasted along with the meat but not too strong to overpower

➡ You can keep spooning the marinade over the meat that you are frying, grilling, or roasting

Sweet Yummies

Introductory comments

Here you'll find pastries and muffins and chocolate slice, and ways to change them as you want. Playing around with these Cooking Catalysts will continue to increase your confidence as you exercise your freedom to choose.

Among the Cooking Catalysts here you'll learn that pastry uses half the amount of butter to the flour/grain and then you'll see how many other sweet treats start the same way:

<u>Welsh cakes:</u> Adds sugar and spice so a sweeter mix
<u>Flapjacks:</u> Adds oats for a crunchier appeal
<u>Fruit and Nut Slice:</u> Adds a middle layer of fruit/nuts
<u>Crumble:</u> Extra flour to ensure a crumbly topping

And I'll show you how to make a home baked Chocolate Celebration Cake to eat just 10 minutes after you first thought of it!

Be creative in your choices, bold on your adventures, and welcoming of all the unexpected moments that present themselves in all kinds of unexpected ways!

Set yourself free to create **Your Own** eats!

A note on flour

Plain flour and self raising flour are cake flours. Self raising flour already has the raising agent and a little salt in it. If you are substituting plain or all purpose flour for self raising flour then add 1 teaspoon of baking powder for each cup of flour.

A note on beating

Beating a mixture is the act of turning a spoon round in the mix as fast as possible (or use an electric mixer). This whips in some air which helps the cake to rise.

A note on butter

Some people prefer to use butter and some people prefer to substitute margarine or other fats. When you read butter, you choose for yourself whether you will use butter or margarine.

Rich Pastry Pies
Makes 2 large pies with lids

Gather up
√ Flour, 6¼ cups
√ Sugar, ½ cup
√ Butter, 2¼ cups
√ Eggs, 2
√ Water to bind
√ Salt, ¼ teaspoon if wanted

Go for it
➡ Cut butter into small pieces and rub into flour
➡ Stir in sugar
➡ Mix eggs with a little water and stir into flour
➡ Gently knead into a dough adding more water if necessary
➡ Roll out to ½ cm/¼ inch thick on a floured board

To make large fruit pies:
➡ Place the pie dish upside down on the pastry and cut out a circle slightly larger than the dish
➡ Line pie dish with this pastry
➡ Fill dish with fruit
➡ Sprinkle fruit with sugar if you want
➡ Re-roll leftover bits of pastry
➡ Cut a slightly smaller round for the top
➡ Wet the edges of the bottom pie crust then put the pie crust lid on top, pressing edges to seal
➡ Prick top of pie with a fork and cook in hot oven for 30 minutes or until pie is browned

Pie and pastry variations

⇒ <u>Basic pastry</u>: Use 3 cups flour, 1 cup of butter and water to bind

⇒ <u>Small Jam Tarts</u>: Cut out rounds of pastry dough to fit tart tins, press pastry into tart tins and put a teaspoon of jam in each. Cook in medium oven for 10-15 minutes

⇒ <u>Jam Tart Cakes</u>: A quantity of the Just Cake mixture will cover 12 small tarts. Put equal size spoonfuls of mixture onto each of the 12 jam tarts before cooking. Cook in medium oven for 15-20 minutes

Chat

-Bread dough benefits from firm handling, pastry dough prefers light handling.

-For small tarts, instead of rolling out pastry and cutting out small circles to line tart tins you can make small balls of pastry dough and press these into the tins to make tart cases.

Picau ar y Maen - Welsh Cakes

Gather up
✓ Self raising flour, 3 cups
✓ Sugar, ¾ cup
✓ Butter, 1 cup
✓ Egg, 1
✓ Milk, 2 TABLESPOONS
✓ Currants, ½ cup
✓ Mixed spice, ½ teaspoon

Go for it
➡ Cut butter into small pieces and rub into flour
➡ Add dry ingredients
➡ Add wet ingredients
➡ Roll out to ½ cm/¼ inch thick on a floured board
➡ Cut into cookie size rounds
➡ Cook on greased griddle or frying pan for 3 minutes each side
➡ When cooked, sprinkle with sugar

Chat
-The Welsh name for griddle is Maen.
-For mixed spice, allspice can be substituted or make you own mixed spice with cinnamon, a little nutmeg, and a little of ground cloves.
-Experiment by cooking Welsh Cake rounds on greased baking sheets in a medium oven for 15 minutes. Very different result and very tasty too!

Oatmeal Flapjacks

Gather up

✓ Butter, 1 cup
✓ Golden syrup/treacle/molasses/honey, ½ cup
✓ Oats, 4½ cups
✓ Sugar, 1 cup

Go for it

➡ Melt butter with syrup in a saucepan
➡ Stir in oats and sugar
➡ Press mixture into a greased pan
  (23cm/9 inches by 30cm/12 inches)
➡ Cook in medium oven for 20 minutes
➡ Cut and remove from pan while warm

Variation

Can add ½ cup dried fruit or chocolate chips to mixture before cooking, or the finished cold flapjacks can be dipped in melted chocolate.

Chat

-To remove cold flapjack more easily from the pan, put pan back in oven for 5 minutes to warm.

Sweet Slice

Gather up
- ✓ Oats, 3 cups
- ✓ Sugar, 1 cup
- ✓ Self raising flour, 1½ cups
- ✓ Butter, 1 cup
- ✓ Eggs, 2 beaten
- ✓ Fruit, 2 cups, (sliced bananas or fruit of choice)
- ✓ Nuts, ½ cup chopped (optional)

Go for it
➡ Mix all dry ingredients together
➡ Stir in melted butter, it is crumbly at this stage
➡ Mix to a stiff dough with eggs
➡ Divide into two
➡ Grease a pan (23cm/9 inches square)
➡ Press half the mixture into the pan
➡ Cover with finely sliced bananas/apples/dates and nuts
➡ Spread remainder of mixture on top and press down firmly
➡ Cook in medium oven for 20 to 30 minutes until golden brown
➡ Cut into fingers while warm, leave to cool in pan

Chat
-If cooked in a metal pan then remove once cool, otherwise the acidic fruit may react with the metal and discolour the cake.

Fruit Crumble

A fruit crumble is made up of two parts, the fruit base and the crumble topping.

Gather up - For the Fruit Base
√ 4 cups of fruit for 12 people

Go for it
➡ Wash fruit, peel and chop
➡ Put fruit in a saucepan with a little water
➡ Cook fruit until soft
➡ Drain excess water, put fruit into crumble dish and if the fruit has not been sugared already, sprinkle 1-2 TABLESPOONS of sugar on the fruit

Gather up - For Crumble Topping for about 12 people
√ Flour, 3 cups
√ Sugar, 1 cup
√ Butter, ¾ cup

Go for it
➡ Stir flour and sugar together
➡ Melt butter
➡ Stir melted butter into flour mix. Will be lumpy and lumpy is good here!
➡ Check fruit is the sweetness you want and then sprinkle crumble topping onto fruit
➡ Cook in medium oven for 30 minutes until brown
➡ Sprinkle a little sugar on top before serving if you want a sweeter dessert

Count Yourself In - Let's Eat!

Chat

-If you forget to sugar the fruit then sprinkle a bit extra on top of the crumble and then when serving offer the bowl of sugar to those eating saying politely, "For those of you with a sweet tooth!!"

-Can use fresh fruit or tinned fruit or a combination (be creative) can substitute up to ¼ total fruit with dried fruit (using more dried fruit makes base very dry).

-If using apples and/or pears then these need to be cooked first.   Soft fruits such as blackberries, redcurrants, blackcurrants, gooseberries, raspberries, do not need cooking before use.

-Rhubarb can be cooked.   It does not need water, though adding a little water to cover bottom of pan helps it cook gently and evenly! Simmer until soft.

-Can substitute in some oats for a more crunchy topping, replace 1 volume quantity of flour with two volumes of oats -- so if you take out ½ cup of flour put in 1 cup of oats.

Just Cake - Syrup Sponge

Gather up

✓ Sugar, ½ cup
✓ Butter, ½ cup (faster if butter is softened)
✓ Vanilla flavouring (optional)
✓ Egg, 1
✓ Milk, 2 TABLESPOONS
✓ Flour, 1 cup

Go for it

➡ Beat sugar and butter
➡ Add egg and vanilla
➡ Stir in flour alternately with milk

Either

➡ Find a microwaveable bowl that is at least twice the volume of the cake mixture
➡ Grease bowl
➡ Put two TABLESPOONS of syrup/molasses in bowl
➡ Cover with sponge mixture
➡ Microwave for 4 minutes

Or

➡ Put syrup and sponge mix into an ovenproof dish
➡ Cook 30 minutes in medium oven

Fast and Fun Celebration Cakes

Go for it

➡ Make a chocolate version of Just Cake above by adding 1 TABLESPOON of cocoa powder and possibly a little more milk if mixture seems dry

Either

➡ Put cake mixture into greased bowl and cook in microwave for 4 minutes. Turn out

Or

➡ Put cake mixture into greased ovenproof round mixing bowl and cook in medium oven for about 30 minutes. Turn out

➡ Serve as fresh as possible

Chat

-The attraction of this celebration cake is that it can be made in the microwave so quickly and if in a hurry, the cake can be served without icing and a celebration candle simply stuck in the top of the round mound. Start to finish less than 10 minutes!

-Two spoonfuls of drinking chocolate usually contain about 1 spoonful of cocoa powder and 1 spoonful sugar. So, if substituting drinking chocolate for cocoa powder take this into account by increasing the amount of chocolate powder and decreasing the amount of sugar.

Hedgehog Celebration Cake

Cover with chocolate butter cream and use your imagination to create a hedgehog. Just pull out butter cream into a smooth pointed snout with a cherry, chocolate button, or raisin on the end. Use sweets or raisins for eyes. Use fork to pull up butter cream on body for prickles or use chocolate buttons for prickles.

Tortoise Celebration Cake

Cover with chocolate butter cream and use half a mini chocolate roll or other suitable chocolate snack bars for head and legs, and sweets or raisins for eyes. Pull out butter cream at one end to shape a small tail.

Football Celebration Cake

Cover with chocolate butter cream and put the ball markings on with raisins or other sweets.

Your choice from a round start

Make anything else that can be created from a round start.

Combo Cake

Perhaps a banana bread, perhaps a carrot cake
or - your Combo choice

Gather up

✓ Oil/melted butter, 1 cup
✓ Sugar, 2 cups
✓ Eggs, 3
✓ Vanilla flavouring, 2 teaspoons
✓ Self raising flour, 3 cups
✓ Fruit or vegetables, 3 cups, mashed, chopped, or grated (try peaches, banana, apple, or carrots)
✓ Nuts, 1 cup (optional)
✓ Coconut, 1 cup (optional)

Go for it

➡ Mix ingredients in order listed
➡ Put into a greased bundt (large ring) pan or 2 or 3 smaller pans
➡ Cook one hour (more or less depending on size of cakes) in medium oven

Quick cream cheese frosting for your Combo Cake

Gather up

✓ Cream cheese, ⅓ cup
✓ Fruit juice, 1 teaspoon (optional)
✓ Icing sugar, 1½ cups

Go for it

➡ Beat cream cheese until soft
➡ Add juice
➡ Gradually add icing sugar
➡ Spread frosting on top of the cake

Chat

-Using a bundt (ring) pan avoids a soggy middle as there is no middle!! If you are using other shaped pans, make at least two cakes rather than one very large cake if you want to be sure the cake cooks well in the middle.

-This cake is made with oil or melted butter making this cake a fast mix.

-If adding coconut or cocoa powder you may want a little extra liquid.

-Dusting the greased pan with a little flour before putting in the cake mixture makes it easier to remove the cooked cake.

The Icing on the Cakes!

Go for it - Simple icing
➡ Put a cup of icing sugar into a bowl. Add water slowly by the teaspoonful until you have an icing that can be spread on a cake!!

Go for it - Butter Icing
➡ Soften ⅓ cup butter in a bowl and gradually mix in 1 cup icing sugar adding enough warm milk or water for desired consistency

Butter icing variations
➡ <u>Vanilla butter icing</u>: Add some vanilla flavouring
➡ <u>Coffee butter icing</u>: Put 1 teaspoon of instant coffee granules into cup. Add 2-3 teaspoons boiling water to dissolve granules. Add to icing
➡ <u>Chocolate butter icing</u>: Stir in 3 teaspoons of cocoa powder or drinking chocolate

Go for it - Whipped fresh cream and yoghurt
➡ Use equal quantities of cream and yoghurt, whip cream until thick and stir in yoghurt

Chat
-Icing sugar is also referred to as powdered sugar.

Go for it - Everyday chocolate icing

➡ Use ½ cup melted chocolate, add ¼ cup milk and ¼ cup icing sugar

Go for it - Luxury chocolate icing

➡ Use melted chocolate mixed with an equal amount of unwhipped fresh cream

Go for it - Cream cheese frosting

➡ Mix together 2 cups cream cheese, ½ cup softened butter, 3 cups of icing sugar, and 1 teaspoon lemon juice. Add more icing sugar for a stiffer frosting

Chat

-Chocolate can be melted in a bowl sitting over a pan of boiling water. Bowl must not touch the water. Care must be taken to ensure the chocolate melts slowly into a smooth runny consistency. Once it is beginning to melt turn off the heat and leave chocolate over the hot water, stirring it gently.

-Alternatively, chocolate can be melted in the microwave. Start with 20 seconds and work up until chocolate is melted.

Just Cookies

Gather up

- ✓ Butter, 1 cup
- ✓ Sugar, 1½ cups
- ✓ Eggs, 2
- ✓ Vanilla flavouring, 2 teaspoons
- ✓ Self raising flour, 2½ cups
- ✓ Chocolate pieces or other additions, 2 cups

Go for it

➡ Beat butter, sugar and vanilla together
➡ Beat in eggs one at a time
➡ Stir in flour
➡ Add chocolate pieces or other additions

➡ Drop a TABLESPOON of cookie mix for each cookie onto ungreased baking sheets leaving a little space between each cookie
➡ Cook cookies in medium oven for 10-12 minutes or until golden brown
➡ Cool for two minutes then remove from baking sheets

Chat

–If you prefer, cookies can be made in one large pan and cut into bars when cooled. This uses less pan space than the individual cookies but needs a bit longer in the oven, 20-25 minutes.

Cookie variations

➡ 2 cups Smarties, M&Ms, or chocolate buttons
➡ 1 cup of raisins and 1 cup oats
➡ 1 cup peanut butter and 1 cup soft brown sugar (add these into the mix before adding the flour)
➡ 1 cup applesauce and 1 cup raisins
➡ 1 cup grated carrots and 1 cup pecans
➡ 1 cup of sunflower seeds and 1 cup of...
➡ You get the idea.. This Choice is Yours!

Chat

–Cookies are made chewy by the large quantity of sugar and by undercooking them slightly. So if you reduce the sugar your cookies will probably be less chewy.

–Reducing the chocolate chips just means less of those chocolate bits in each bite!

–Brown sugar gives a rich flavour and also a slightly chewier cookie.

Muffins

Gather up

✓ Flour, 5 cups
✓ Sugar, ½ cup
✓ Oil, ½ cup
✓ Eggs, 2
✓ Milk, 2 cups
✓ Dry additions of choice, up to 3 cups

Go for it

➡ Mix dry ingredients together in a large bowl
➡ Mix wet ingredients together in a medium bowl
➡ Put wet ingredients into dry ingredients, and mix gently
➡ Fill 24 greased muffin tins and, if you want, sprinkle sugar, cinnamon, or nuts on top of muffins
➡ Cook in hot oven for 20 minutes

Chat

–If you are adding any liquid variations, such as water, juice or yoghurt, then substitute for all or part of the milk.
–This is another great place to play around as there is such a wide range of possibilities to add, including leaving out most of the sugar and adding in something savoury like a little cheese.

Chocolate Finale in Three

Chocolate Upside Down Adventure - in a Bowl

Gather up - Cake
✓ Butter, ½ cup
✓ Milk, ¾ cup
✓ Self raising flour, 1½ cups
✓ Sugar, 1½ cups
✓ Cocoa powder, 2 TABLESPOONS

Gather up - Topping
✓ Sugar, 1 cup (brown sugar gives a richer sauce)
✓ Cocoa powder, 2 TABLESPOONS
✓ Boiling water, 4 cups

Go for it
➡ Heat butter and milk gently in saucepan until butter melts
➡ Mix flour, sugar and cocoa powder together in a bowl
➡ Add butter and milk to flour mixture and stir
➡ Pour mixture into a greased ovenproof bowl
➡ Only fill ovenproof bowl ⅓ full
➡ Mix sugar and cocoa powder and sprinkle over mixture
➡ And lastly pour boiling water over mixture
➡ Cook in medium oven for 45 minutes

Chat

-This is a great dessert to make if you have no eggs. The Chocolate Upside Down Adventure needs no eggs.

-Also, if you are short of cocoa powder you can omit it from the topping. You get a less chocolaty sauce but it is still good especially if made richer by using brown sugar.

-If this dessert seems a bit gooey when served, that's OK, there are no eggs in the dessert so there is no problem that it is a bit undercooked. Can be renamed 'Squishy Chocolate Upside Down Adventure' when necessary!

-After cooking, the cake is on top with a sauce underneath - hence the name.

Chocolate Slice

Gather up

- √ Self raising flour, 2 cups
- √ Sugar, 2 cups
- √ Butter, 1 cup
- √ Cocoa powder, 4 TABLESPOONS
- √ Water, 1 cup
- √ Eggs, 2
- √ Yoghurt, ½ cup (can substitute milk)
- √ Vanilla, 1 teaspoon

Go for it

- ➡ Mix flour and sugar in a large bowl
- ➡ Mix yoghurt, eggs, and vanilla in a small bowl
- ➡ Put butter and cocoa powder in a saucepan with the water and heat gently until butter melts
- ➡ Bring butter mix to the boil
- ➡ Stir this melted butter mix into flour
- ➡ Stir the egg mix into flour mix
- ➡ Pour mixture into one or two large greased pans
- ➡ Cook in hot oven for 15 minutes

Icing for Chocolate Slice

Gather up

✓ Butter, ½ cup
✓ Cocoa powder, 4 TABLESPOONS
✓ Milk, 6 TABLESPOONS
✓ Icing sugar, 3 cups

Go for it

➡ Put butter, cocoa powder, and milk in a saucepan
➡ Heat gently
➡ Gradually bring to the boil
➡ Remove from heat
➡ Stir in about 3 cups icing sugar (until icing is the texture you want)

➡ As soon as cake is out of oven, drizzle icing on it. Decorate with nuts if you want

Real Deal Chocolate Brownies

Gather up

- √ Sugar, 1 cup
- √ Plain flour, ¾ cup
- √ Butter, ½ cup softened
- √ Cocoa powder, 5 TABLESPOONS
- √ Salt, ½ teaspoon
- √ Eggs, 2
- √ Vanilla flavouring, 1 TABLESPOON (optional)
- √ Nuts or dried fruit, ½ cup chopped (optional)

Go for it

- ➡ Put all ingredients into a large bowl and beat together. Stir in nuts or dried fruit if you want
- ➡ Grease a 20 cm/9 inches square baking pan (or other pan with similar area)
- ➡ Pour chocolate cake into greased pan
- ➡ Decorate with nuts if you want
- ➡ Cook 30 minutes in medium oven
- ➡ Take out of oven and leave in pan to cool
- ➡ Cut into pieces and leave in pan for serving

Chat

-This quantity cuts nicely into 9 or 12 pieces so resist the urge to split it between two!!

-Using a little simple calculation you can make twice the quantity next time.

-What makes these Brownies inexpensive compared with other Brownies is the use of cocoa powder instead of chocolate or chocolate chips.

-You can replace the butter with oil.

-If you have no cocoa powder or want a change, make Blondies instead of Brownies. Omit the cocoa powder (and replace this dry ingredient with a little extra flour) and if you want, add another flavour such as orange/lemon zest or coffee flavouring.

-Can be served alone or as a dessert with cream, fruit, ice cream, or yoghurt.

This Choice is Yours!

So you've come to the back of the book

This book is about creating remarkable results from ordinary things

The adventure begins in a cookbook and moves out into life

Count Yourself In

For More Notes on Your Remarkable Adventures

For More Notes on Your Remarkable Adventures

Count Yourself In - Let's Eat
More than a way of cooking, it's a way of life

Made in the USA
Charleston, SC
09 May 2013